AUSTRALIAN SOAP OPERA WRITERS

Peter Pinne, Richard Lane, Reg Watson, Liddy Holloway, Shane Porteous, Don Battye, David Sale, Patrea Smallacombe, Betty Quin

 BOOKS LLC

Publication Data:

Title: Australian Soap Opera Writers

Subtitle: Peter Pinne, Richard Lane, Reg Watson, Liddy Holloway, Shane Porteous, Don Battye, David Sale, Patrea Smallacombe, Betty Quin

Published by: Books LLC, Memphis, Tennessee, USA in 2010

Copyright (chapters): http://creativecommons.org/licenses/by-sa/3.0

Online edition: http://en.wikipedia.org/wiki/Category:Australian_soap_opera_writers

Contact the publisher: http://booksllc.net/contactus.cfm

CONTENTS

Introduction

The online edition of this book is at http://booksllc.net/?q=Category:Australian% 5Fsoap%5Fopera%5Fwriters. It's hyperlinked and may be updated. Where we have recommended related pages, you can read them at http://booksllc.net/?q= followed by the page's title. Most entries in the book's index also have a dedicated page at http://booksllc.net/?q= followed by the index entry.

Each chapter in this book ends with a URL to a hyperlinked online version. Use the online version to access related pages, websites, footnote URLs. You can click the history tab on the online version to see a list of the chapter's contributors. While we have included photo captions in the book, due to copyright restrictions you can only view the photos online. You also need to go to the online edition to view some formula symbols or foreign language characters.

The online version of this book is part of Wikipedia, a multilingual, web-based encyclopedia.

Wikipedia is written collaboratively. Since its creation in 2001, Wikipedia has grown rapidly into one of the largest reference web sites, attracting nearly 68 million visitors monthly. There are more than 91,000 active contributors working on more than 15 million articles in more than 270 languages. Every day, hundreds of thousands of active from around the world collectively make tens of thousands of edits and create thousands of new articles.

After a long process of discussion, debate, and argument, articles gradually take on a neutral point of view reached through consensus. Additional editors expand and contribute to articles and strive to achieve balance and comprehensive coverage. Wikipedia's intent is to cover existing knowledge which is verifiable from other sources. The ideal Wikipedia article is well-written, balanced, neutral, and encyclopedic, containing comprehensive, notable, verifiable knowledge.

Wikipedia is open to a large contributor base, drawing a large number of editors from diverse backgrounds. This allows Wikipedia to significantly reduce regional and cultural bias found in many other publications, and makes it very difficult for any group to censor and impose bias. A large, diverse editor base also provides access and breadth on subject matter that is otherwise inaccessible or little documented.

Think you can improve the book? If so, simply go to the online version and suggest changes. If accepted, your additions could appear in the next edition!

BETTY QUIN

Betty Quin is an Australian script writer and series script editor who has contributed to numerous soap operas in her native Australia (e.g. *The Young Doctors*,
Sons and Daughters, *A Country Practice, Prisoner* and *Neighbours*). At one time,
she also ran her own theatre company in Adelaide. She is the Aunt of the Australian
born, *Coronation Street* and EastEnders script writer, Patrea Smallacombe.

Websites (URLs online)

  o Betty Quin on IMDB

A hyperlinked version of this chapter is at http://booksllc.net?q=Betty%5FQuin

2

DAVID SALE

David Sale is an Australian-based author and television screenwriter. He has contributed to many TV drama series, provided special material for Australia's leading entertainers, and has worked as producer, director, actor and journalist.

He is perhaps best known as creator, writer and script editor of the highly influential television soap opera *Number 96*. Before that, he was Executive Producer of the satirical weekly comedy *The Mavis Bramston Show*. Both of these series were highly popular in their day and still rank amongst the most famous and influential programs to have appeared on Australian television.

His first two novels, written between TV assignments, were *Come to Mother* and *The Love Bite*. These were published in London in hardback in the 1970s and both were bought by Hollywood. *Come to Mother* was made into the television film *Live Again, Die Again* (1974).

Television interrupted this flow of books, but in the 1990s Sale resumed his career as an author with *Twisted Echoes* (1993) (HODDER HEADLINE); *Scorpion's Kiss* (1995) (PAN MACMILLAN) and *Hidden Agenda* (1996) (PAN MACMILLAN).

He later tackled Musical Theatre for the first time with his co-written (book and lyrics) version of Sumner Locke Elliott's novel *Careful, He Might Hear You.*

Books

- *Come to Mother* (1971) (W.H. ALLEN) (ISBN 0-491-00317-X)
- *The Love Bite* (1972) (W.H. ALLEN)
- *Chiller* (1983, "based on *The Love Bite*") (SPHERE) (ISBN 0-7221-7625-2)
- *Antidote* (1991) (BANTAM) (ISBN 1-86359-027-7)
- *Twisted Echoes* (1993) (HODDER HEADLINE) (ISBN 0-74724083-3)
- *Scorpion's Kiss* (1995) (PAN MACMILLAN) (ISBN 0-33027497-X)
- *Hidden Agenda* (1996) (PAN MACMILLAN) (ISBN 0-33035737-9)

Websites (URLs online)

- David Sale at the Internet Movie Database

A hyperlinked version of this chapter is at http://booksllc.net?q=David%5FSale

3

DON BATTYE

Don Battye (born 29 September 1938) is an Australian born composer and television producer.

Life

He was a producer on several Australian television series for Crawford Productions including soap opera *The Box* in 1976-77, and police procedural drama series *Bluey* (1976) and *Homicide*.

Peter Pinne and he wrote musicals which premiered at the Alexander Theatre Monash University, from 1973 to 1980. [1]

He later worked for the Reg Grundy Organisation as producer on such programmes as police procedural drama series *Bellamy* (1981), and soap operas *Sons and Daughters* (1982),[2] *Waterloo Station* (1983), *Possession* (1985), and *Neighbours*. [3] Battye co-composed the famous theme song to *Sons and Daughters* with Peter Pinne.

With Pinne in the late 1990s he set up the record label *Bayview* on leaving the Grundy Organisation.[4] He now produces and composes music from the Philippines where he now resides.

He and Brian Kavanagh wrote the screenplay *City's Child*.[5]

Books

- Peter N. Pinne and Don Battye. (1988). *A bunch of ratbags*. Montmorency, Vic.: Yackandandah. ISBN 0731638972. (Adapted from the novel by William Dick) [6]
- Peter N. Pinne and Don Battye. (1981). *Caroline, a musical play based on the life and times of Caroline Chisholm*. Brisbane Playlab Press,. ISBN 0908156138.
- Peter N. Pinne and Don Battye. (1989). *Red, white and boogie*. Montmorency, Vic. Yackandandah,. ISBN 0868050717.

References (URLs online)

- 1. http://www.davidspicer.com/ppanddb.htm
- 2. http://www.tvmem.com/DATA/A-Z/S/SONSANDD/SONSANDD.html
- 3. http://perfectblend.net/features/interview-battye.htm
- 4. http://www.perfectblend.net/features/interview-pinne.htm
- 5. http://www.film.com/movies/a-citys-child/21092146
- 6. http://www.magnormos.com/mtrp_abor_about.htm

Websites (URLs online)

- Don Battye at the Internet Movie Database
- "DON BATTYE", *doollee*

A hyperlinked version of this chapter is at http://booksllc.net?q=Don%5FBattye

4

LIDDY HOLLOWAY

Elizabeth Brenda "Liddy" Holloway (March 27, 1945 December 29, 2004) was a New Zealand actress.

Born in Wellington, New Zealand, the daughter of a politician, Phil Holloway, Liddy Holloway originally worked as a journalist. She switched to acting and had a long career in the theater. She also acted in Australia in the early 1980s, with acting roles in feature films *Squizzy Taylor* and *The Clinic*. She also acted on Australian television, appearing in guest roles in several episodes of soap opera *Prisoner*, a series for which she also wrote some scripts.

Holloway moved to Los Angeles briefly in 1990 to give Hollywood a try, but did not stay long. She eventually garnered international attention for her recurring role as Hercules' mother on the syndicated adventure series, *Hercules: The Legendary Journeys*, a role she played intermittently from 1995 to 1998.

Holloway also found wide recognition in her home country through her 1992-1998 lead role of Alex McKenna in the popular soap opera *Shortland Street*. Holloway was also a writer for the series. She was the first person to champion making the book *The Whale Rider* into a feature film. Holloway fought with the Film Commission because she wanted a writing credit for her work on the 2002 feature.

In 2002 Holloway portrayed Dorthy Moxley, mother of murder victim Martha Moxley, in the American television movie *Murder in Greenwich*, which, although set in Connecticut, was filmed in New Zealand.

Death

On December 29, 2004, Liddy Holloway died, aged 59, from liver cancer. She was survived by three children, Francesca Holibar, Mark Harlen, and actor/ musician Joel Tobeck, who appeared with her on *Shortland Street*.

Websites (URLs online)

  o Liddy Holloway at the Internet Movie Database
  o Shortland Street interview

A hyperlinked version of this chapter is at http://booksllc.net?q=Liddy%5FHolloway

5

PATREA SMALLACOMBE

Patrea Smallacombe (born 1961, Adelaide, Australia) is a prolific Australian writer and series script editor who contributed to numerous soap operas in her native Australia including *The Young Doctors*, *Prisoner*, *Neighbours* and *A Country Practice* before moving to the United Kingdom in 1987. Since then she has written for many high profile shows including *Emmerdale*, *Brookside*, *Family Affairs*, *The Bill* and also two separate stints penning scripts for the top rated ITV1 soap opera, *Coronation Street*. Her aunt, is the equally prolific Australian television series script writer, Betty Quin.

As of May 2007, Smallacombe had joined the scriptwriting team of EastEnders.

A hyperlinked version of this chapter is at http://booksllc.net?q=Patrea% 5FSmallacombe

6

PETER PINNE

Peter Pinne (born 27 May 1937) is an Australian-born writer and composer.

Pinne started working as a television executive for the Reg Grundy organisation. Firstly, as Head of Production from 1980, later rising to become a Senior Vice President of the company. During this period, he worked on numerous shows including The Young Doctors, The Restless Years and Neighbours. In addition, he also famously co-composed the theme tune to Sons and Daughters (Australian TV series). In 1992, he was also responsible for overseeing the production of Dangerous Women, an American series based loosely on the popular Prisoner format. However, the show was not a huge success running to only 52 one hour episodes. Thereafter, he also travelled to a number of Latin American countries where he was responsible for overseeing the production of local versions of some of Grundy's most successful hits. He left the Grundy organisation in the late 1990s in order to set up his own record label, Bayview, with fellow former Australian television producer, Don Battye and now writes and composes music.

Stage Musicals

Since the late 1950s, Peter Pinne (variously working in collaboration with Don Battye, Ray Kolle and/or John-Michael Howson) has been one of the most prolific creators of original Australian stage musicals. Examples include:

- o *All Saint's Day* (1960) - based around Australian Rules Football
- o *Don't tell Helena* (1962) - the misadventures of a society girl employed by a department store
- o *A Bunch of Ratbags* (1966) - a rock musical set in the 1950s, adapted from the novel by William Dick
- o *It happened in Tanjablanca* (1968); later revised as *Red, White and Boogie* (1974) - a murder mystery set in the 1940s
- o *The Computer/Love's Travelling Saleman* (1970) - a double bill of one-act "pop operas"
- o *Caroline* (1971) - based on the life of Caroline Chisholm
- o *Sweet Fanny Adams* (1974) - the story of two rival whorehouses in 1930s Sydney
- o *A bit o' petticoat* (1984) - based on "The Torrents" by Australian playwright Oriel Gray
- o *Pyjamas in Paradise* (2005) - based on the popular "pyjama parties" held in Surfers Paradise in the 1950s
- o *Suddenly Single* (2007)

Most of these musicals were originally performed as amateur or semi-professional productions. Although private demonstration recordings of the scores are known to exist, few of the shows had commercial cast albums released. A song from *A Bunch of Ratbags* was released as a single, cover versions of two songs from *The Computer* and *Love's Travelling Salesman* were included on a 1970 compilation LP entitled *Australian Musicals Now*, and a studio recording of selections from *Red, White and Boogie* and *Sweet Fanny Adams* was released in 1983 on Don Battye's Trigpoint label. The only stage production to generate a complete original cast recording was *Caroline*; the original LP was released in 1971 and subsequently re-issued on CD (by London-based label Dress Circle Records) in 1998.

Although all of Pinne's musicals were successful in their original productions, few of them have been mounted since. As mentioned above, the 1968 show *It happened in Tanjablanca* was revived in 1974, in a substantially revised version entitled *Red White and Boogie*. The following year, a suburban amateur theatre company in Melbourne staged a production of *Caroline*. More recently, *A Bunch of Ratbags* was revived in 2005 by Magnormos Productions, which resulted in the release of a "premiere" cast recording. In 2007, Magnormos Productions staged a 30-minute workshop production of Pinne's latest musical, *Suddenly Single*, which was written in collaboration with Paul Dellit.

In the mid-1990s, Pinne and Battye also wrote a stage musical adaptation of the cult 1970s Australian television series, *Prisoner: Cell Block H*. Ironically, the show was first produced in England (where the original programme had become more popular than it was in its native land), in a lavish West End production that starred Lily Savage and original TV cast member Maggie Kirkpatrick, reprising her role as Joan "The Freak" Ferguson.

In addition, Pinne and Battye co-wrote a number of pantomime-like musicals especially for children, which were produced at the Alexander Theatre at Monash University during the 1970s. Mostly based on popular fairy tales, these shows included:

- *The Shoemaker and the Elves* (1975)
- *Jack and the Beanstalk* (1976)
- *Billabong Bill'* (1976)
- *The Little Tin Soldier* (1977)
- *The Emperor's New Clothes* (1978)
- *Rumpelstiltskin*
- *Beauty and the Beast*

Books

- *Australian performers, Australian performances a discography from film, TV, theatre, radio and concert, 1897-1985* (1987) (ISBN 0-72418208-X)
- Albert Moran ; with additional research by Peter Pinne (1993). *Moran's guide to Australian TV series*. North Ryde, N.S.W. Australian Film Television and Radio School distributed in Australia and New Zealand by Allen & Unwin. ISBN 0-64-218462-3.
- music and lyrics by Peter N. Pinne ; book and lyrics by Don Battye. Adapted from the novel by William Dick' (1988). *A bunch of ratbags*. Montmorency, Vic. Yackandandah. ISBN 0-73-163897-2.
- Peter N. Pinne and Don Battye. (1981). *Caroline, a musical play based on the life and times of Caroline Chisholm*. Brisbane Playlab Press,. ISBN 0-90-815613-8.
- Peter N. Pinne and Don Battye. (1989). *Red, white and boogie*. Montmorency, Vic. Yackandandah,. ISBN 0-86-805071-7.
- book and lyrics by Ray Kolle ; music by Peter Pinne; Based on 'The Torrents' by Oriel Gray (1992). *A bit o' petticoat a musical*. Montmorency, Vic. Yackandandah,. ISBN 0-86-805085-7.

Websites (URLs online)

- Peter Pinne at the Internet Movie Database

A hyperlinked version of this chapter is at http://booksllc.net?q=Peter%5FPinne

7

REG WATSON

Reginald James "Reg" Watson OAM is an Australian television producer, best known for creating soap operas like *Prisoner* and *Neighbours*.

Career

Reg started his career as an actor at the age of sixteen on Australian radio, before moving to the UK in 1955. He soon was hired by ATV, and in 1956 joined Ned Sherrin and Noele Gordon in Birmingham to set up and launch ATV Midlands. Reg's job was as Head Of Light Entertainment.

In this role he created many programmes for the station with his first big hit being the live daily chat show, *Lunchbox*. It ran from 1956 to 1964, creating over 3000 editions. In 1958 Reg submitted a proposal for a new Midlands based soap opera to ATV, however it wasn't until 1964 that Lew Grade, head of the station, granted approval for the soap. It was to be the first full length daily serial in the UK, it was called 'The Midland Road.'

Reg later changed the soap's name to *Crossroads* and he took the show, along with its creators Hazel Adair and Peter Ling, to audiences of 18 million. After ten years producing *Crossroads*, and eighteen years at ATV he decided to return to Australia in 1973. Upon his return home he took up the post of head of drama at Reg Grundy Productions. Thanks to his hit British soap, he was able to create many more memorable productions including *The Young Doctors*, *Glenview High*, *The Restless Years* and *Sons and Daughters*. *The Young Doctors* and *Sons and Daughters* later aired in the UK. The fame that he earned from *Sons and Daughters* allowed his idea for *Neighbours* to be picked up by the Seven Network in 1985. After being cancelled by Seven that year due to low ratings it switched to the Ten Network at the start of 1986 and slowly its ratings climbed. Currently, the show still airs on Network Ten and is the longest-running drama series in Australian television history. At the 47th Annual TV Week Logie Awards held on 1 May 2005, *Neighbours* became the 22nd inductee into the TV Week Hall of Fame.

Watson also dabbled in television production in America, producing *Dangerous Women*, a short-lived soap opera based on the Australian *Prisoner* series.

Personal life

Watson is a shy man, and rarely gives interviews, he is now happily retired and has not produced any new television drama since 1992. In daily life, Watson is a caring, humorous, and approachable person.

On 26 January 2010, Watson was appointed an Member of the Order of Australia for service to the media as a pioneer in the creation and production of serial television drama.[1] [2]

References (URLs online)

o 1. "Reg Watson AM". Australian Honours Database. Retrieved 26 January 2010.
o 2. "Neighbours creator Honoured".

A hyperlinked version of this chapter is at http://booksllc.net?q=Reg%5FWatson

8

RICHARD LANE (WRITER)

Richard Lane (19182008) was an Australian writer known particularly for his skillful adaptation of plays and films for radio. He is often called the father of Australian radio drama. His career spanned over 60 years, and he is recognised not only for his writing achievements but for his contribution to the Australian Writers' Guild. He also wrote for television, and was described after his death as "luminary of the Australian radio and television industries".[1]

Life

Richard Lane was born in the Sydney beach suburb of Coogee and went to school in Sydney's northern suburbs at Knox Grammar School in Wahroonga, where "he excelled as an athlete and edited the school magazine".[2]

Lane married a few times, with his last wife being the Australian actor, Lynne Murphy.

Writing career

Lane's first short story was published while he was still at school, and more of his stories were published in magazines in the following year.[2] However, it was in radio drama, still in its infancy when he started, that he found his vocation. His first radio play was *No Escape*.[3]

By the age of 21 Lane had had a number of plays produced by the Australian Broadcasting Commission (ABC) and he was being recognised as "an exciting new talent".[2]

He became senior playwright at Sydney's radio station 2GB, Australia's largest producer of radio drama. He adapted plays into one-hour dramas, and novels into serial form.[2] He wrote and produced the long-running radio serial Dr Paul.[3]

Actors such as Peter Finch appeared in his early plays.

By 1949, he was recognised as Australia's "foremost radio playwright"[2]. He decided at this time to go freelance, and directed as well as wrote radio drama. With the arrival of television in Australian in 1956, he began writing for that medium too. He wrote for the first Australian produced drama series, *Autumn Affair*.[2] He adapted classic works, such as Ibsen's *Hedda Gabler*, into television plays, and Jon Cleary's *You can't see 'round corners* into a serial.

Lane moved to Melbourne and continued to write for television - for such programs as *Bellbird*, *Homicide*, *The Sullivans* and *Carson's Law* - while also writing for radio. He won four Australian Writers Guild (AWGIE) Awards for his work.[2]

In his later career he wrote two books on the history of radio drama in Australia, *The Golden Age of Australian Radio Drama*. These books have been described as "history through biography"[2] and provide a comprehensive record of the actors, writers, producers and directors involved in radio drama at "the time when Australia produced more radio drama than any country in the world".[2]

Besides his writing, Lane is known for the work he did in forming the Australian Writers Guild. He was part of the group which formed it in 1962, [4] and was its Vice-President from 1962-64 and then its third President from 1964-68.[3] He was involved in "setting up state branches for the guild, lobbying for an Australian quota, introducing the AWGIE Awards for writers, and helping establish the Australian Film and Television School".[2] Lane was also committed to developing a standard industry-wide contract for use between writers and the production companies or networks, using British agreements as a model. While there was initial support within the industry, problems occurred over the issue of residuals, particularly with the ABC. The ABC finally signed the Guild's standard contract in the early 1970s.[4]

In 1988, the Guild awarded him a special award for outstanding contribution to the guild. This special award, named Richard Lane Award, has become an annual award that is presented to an AWG member "in recognition of their outstanding service to the Guild"..[1]

Awards

- o 1968: AWGIE (Australian Writers Guild) Award: Major Award for the television adaptation of *You Cant See 'Round Corners*
- o 1975: AWGIE Award: for episode of *Bellbird*
- o 1977: AWGIE Award: for episode of *Bellbird*
- o 1985: AWGIE Award: for Best Radio Adaptation for *Great Expectations*
- o 1988: AWGIE Award (later named The Richard Lane Award): for outstanding contribution to the Guild
- o 1996: ASRA (Australasian Sound Recording Association) Award: for outstanding contributions to radio drama in Australia.

Notes

- o 1. AusLit News June/July 2008
- o 2. Yeldham (2008)
- o 3. *Vale Richard Lane*
- o 4. *History of the AWG 1962-2002*

References (URLs online)

- o *History of the AWG 1962-2002* Accessed: 2008-03-23
- o *Vale Richard Lane* Accessed: 2008-03-23
- o Yeldham, Peter (2008) "Founding father of radio drama: Richard Lane (1918-2008)", in *The Sydney Morning Herald*, 2008-03-11

A hyperlinked version of this chapter is at http://booksllc.net?q=Richard% 5FLane%5F%28writer%29

9

SHANE PORTEOUS

Shane Porteous (born 17 August 1942 in Coleraine, Victoria) is an Australian television character actor, Scriptwriter and Theatre actor.

He remains best known for playing Dr. Terence Elliott in the television drama series *A Country Practice* for its twelve-year run on the Seven Network from 1981 to 1993, a role which he won two logie awards for in 1990 and 1992 respectively. He has also won Awgie awards for various Scriptwriting projects.

Other TV credits include: *Catch Kandy, Homicide, Matlock Police, The Box* in 1974, *Number 96* in 1977, *Glenview High, Neighbours, Home and Away Blue Heelers* and *Heartbreak High*. He has also written scripts for several television series, including *Neighbours* and *Home and Away*, sometimes under the name John Hanlon, And Was honoured for his contribution to scriptwriting and the performing arts in the Queens New Years List of 2001.

Porteous performed in many stage plays, amongst them *Hamlet* and *Death of a Salesman*. He was a regular at the *Q Theatre* in Penrith, New South Wales.

Porteous was also the ambassador for the *Q Theatre*, which was demolished in August 2005 and moved to the Joan Sutherland Performing Arts Centre. [1]

Porteous resides in the village of Medlow Bath in the Blue Mountains in New South Wales. He has a wife, Jenny, and three grown children, Fiona, Polly, and Ben. [2] Shane Porteous has also worked for the Hanna-Barbera Animation Company. As a Theatre actor he has appeared in the play Codgers with Ron Haddrick.

He is referenced in the popular Australian song "I'm so Postmodern" by The Bedroom Philosopher.

References (URLs online)

- o 1. http://www.jspac.com.au/q_theatre_history.php
- o 2. http://acountrypractice.com/Cast/Bios/sporteous.html

Websites (URLs online)

- o Shane Porteous at the Internet Movie Database
- o Wandin Valley Bush Nursing Hospital website

A hyperlinked version of this chapter is at http://booksllc.net?q=Shane%5FPorteous

INDEX